Women Of The New Testament

10 Studies For Individuals Or Groups

Phyllis J. Le Peau

16pt

Read How You Want
LARGE PRINT BOOKS, BRAILLE & DAISY

Copyright Page from the Original Book

InterVarsity Press
P.O. Box 1400, Downers Grove, IL 60515-1426
ivpress.com
email@ivpress.com

P	31	30	29	28	27	26	25	24	23	22	21	20	19	18	17	16
Y	31	30	29	28	27	26	25	24	23	22	21	20	19	18	17	16

TABLE OF CONTENTS

Getting the Most Out of Women of the New Testament

Women in the New Testament are as diverse as women today. I love getting to know them. I am challenged by most to draw closer to God and am warned by a few. I find myself wanting to grow in faith as I observe those who believed God when everything around them screamed of the impossibility of the situation.

I want to be as generous as the New Testament women and to care for others as they did. I am deeply touched by the way Elizabeth graciously received a good gift from God, influencing those around her who saw God's goodness in her life. I am excited by Priscilla's partnership in the gospel with her husband and the contributions that she made to the early church.

The Bible is sometimes accused of being anti-woman. That is not what I see as I look at the women in the New Testament. I see Jesus reaching out to comfort and give hope to women. I see him point out their godly acts to others. He honors their faith and defends their acts of worship and gratitude. In an age when women are regarded as second-class citizens in society and in religious tradition, Jesus esteems them and allows them to play a vital role in his life, death, burial and resurrection.

The Bible also depicts Paul working side-by-side with many women. He allows them to take places of leadership, and he personally benefits from what they offer him. He puts time and energy into dealing with a conflict between two women who had been leaders at his side.

In the early church, women are respected by the apostles and held responsible for their own actions and decisions. Women are taken seriously. Sapphira loses her life because of a decision she made to disobey. The first convert in Philippi is a woman.

As you get to know these women from the New Testament, I hope you too will grow in faith and know God more deeply as you see him in their lives.

Suggestions for Individual Study

1. As you begin each study, pray that God will speak to you through his Word.

2. Read the introduction to the study and respond to the personal reflection question or exercise. This is designed to help you focus on God and on the theme of the study.

3. Each study deals with a particular passage—so that you can delve into the author's meaning in that context. Read and reread the passage to be studied. The questions are written using the language of the New International Version, so you may wish to use that version of

the Bible. The New Revised Standard Version is also recommended.

4. This is an inductive Bible study, designed to help you discover for yourself what Scripture is saying. The study includes three types of questions. *Observation* questions ask about the basic facts: who, what, when, where and how. *Interpretation* questions delve into the meaning of the passage. *Application* questions help you discover the implications of the text for growing in Christ. These three keys unlock the treasures of Scripture.

Write your answers to the questions in the spaces provided or in a personal journal. Writing can bring clarity and deeper understanding of yourself and of God's Word.

5. It might be good to have a Bible dictionary handy. Use it to look up any unfamiliar words, names or places.

6. Use the prayer suggestion to guide you in thanking God for what you have learned and to pray about the applications that have come to mind.

7. You may want to go on to the suggestion under "Now or Later," or you may want to use that idea for your next study.

Suggestions for Members of a Group Study

1. Come to the study prepared. Follow the suggestions for individual study mentioned above. You will find that careful preparation will greatly enrich your time spent in group discussion.

2. Be willing to participate in the discussion. The leader of your group will not be lecturing. Instead, he or she will be encouraging the members of the group to discuss what they have learned. The leader will be asking the questions that are found in this guide.

3. Stick to the topic being discussed. Your answers should be based on the verses which are the focus of the discussion and not on outside authorities such as commentaries or speakers. These studies focus on a particular passage of Scripture. Only rarely should you refer to other portions of the Bible. This allows for everyone to participate in in-depth study on equal ground.

4. Be sensitive to the other members of the group. Listen attentively when they describe what they have learned. You may be surprised by their insights! Each question assumes a variety of answers. Many questions do not have "right" answers, particularly questions that aim at meaning or application. Instead the questions push us to explore the passage more thoroughly.

When possible, link what you say to the comments of others. Also, be affirming whenever you can. This will encourage some of the more hesitant members of the group to participate.

5. Be careful not to dominate the discussion. We are sometimes so eager to express our thoughts that we leave too little opportunity for others to respond. By all means participate! But allow others to also.

6. Expect God to teach you through the passage being discussed and through the other members of the group. Pray that you will have an enjoyable and profitable time together, but also that as a result of the study you will find ways that you can take action individually and/or as a group.

7. Remember that anything said in the group is considered confidential and should not be discussed outside the group unless specific permission is given to do so.

8. If you are the group leader, you will find additional suggestions at the back of the guide.

I

Elizabeth

Receiving God's Goodness

Luke 1:5-25, 39-45, 57-66

Each person in our group wept as Don and Patrice told the story of their lost baby. We had prayed together that God would grant them a child. For a long time we waited patiently and with hope. And we celebrated wildly with ice cream and pickles when finally she conceived! Now, we felt the agony and despair of a dream gone. Would they ever be able to have a child?

GROUP DISCUSSION. When have you had the experience of longing for something for years?

PERSONAL REFLECTION. Reflect on a time in your life when you did not receive something that you longed for deeply. What did you learn about God in that experience?

In this study we will look at how God met Elizabeth in her suffering. *Read Luke 1:5-25.*

1. Looking through the whole passage, what clues do you find about what Elizabeth was like?

_____

2. Note the description of the promised son, John (vv.14-17). What would it be like to discover that you were going to have a son like this?

_____

3. Contrast Zechariah's response to the promise of John's birth (v.18) with Elizabeth's response (v.25).

_____

4. In terms of responses to God's promises, do you think you are more like Elizabeth or Zechariah? Explain.

5. Why do we sometimes not accept good gifts from God or from others?

6. *Read Luke 1:39-45.* The angel Gabriel had informed Mary of Jesus' coming and of Elizabeth's pregnancy. Why do you think it is so important to Mary to get together with Elizabeth?

7. What does this interaction reveal about the relationship between Elizabeth and Mary?

8. How have your faith and obedience to God been affected by other believers?

9. What would be helpful in making this more a part of your experience?

10. *Read Luke 1:57-66.* What did Elizabeth's husband, neighbors and relatives learn about God through this experience of John's birth?

11. Elizabeth's relatives learned about God because she obeyed God and was able to receive God's goodness to her. How have your neighbors and relatives seen God's mercy and grace through your life?

Pray that your eyes will be open to the mercy and grace of God and that your life will be full of praise and thanksgiving to God.

Now or Later

Reflect on how or when it has been difficult for you to believe God and to be a recipient of his good gifts. Journal on each of the times that come to mind. Write about why you think it was difficult to trust God.

Talk to God about what you discover in your journaling.

2

Mary

Believing the Impossible

Luke 1:26-38, 46-56

We often use the phrase "Nothing is impossible with God." Mary, however, is called upon not just to use this phrase, but to believe it.

GROUP DISCUSSION. When do you have trouble believing God?

PERSONAL REFLECTION. In what ways has God demonstrated to you that he is trustworthy?

Gabriel's sign to Mary that God can do anything is the pregnancy of her cousin, Elizabeth. *Read Luke 1:26-38.*

1. Think of yourself as Mary, a teenage girl. Tell the story of the encounter with Gabriel to your best friend.

2. What things was Mary asked to believe?

_____

3. How would you have responded if it were you?

_____

4. How does Mary's question to Gabriel (v.34) contrast with Zechariah's question (v.18)?

_____

5. What do you learn about Mary and her relationship with God in verse 38?

6. How would you like your relationship with God to be more like Mary's?

7. How would Mary's life be complicated by what was going to happen to her?

8. In light of these complications how might she have responded to God?

9. *Read Luke 1:46-56.* What attitudes and feelings toward God does Mary express in these verses?

10. How does Mary see and bring together God's work in history and God's work in her future?

11. Why do you think Mary was able to believe God for the impossible?

_____

12. What steps do you need to take for your response to and faith in God to become more like that of Mary?

Pray that your response to and faith in God will grow.

Now or Later

Write a prayer to God. In it include praise for who he is, gratitude for his work in history—including your own personal history—and thank him for his hope for the future. Thank him for sending Jesus.

3

Herodias

The Fruit of Bitterness

Mark 6:14-29

The author of Hebrews writes about the root of bitterness that springs up and grows a fruit that causes trouble and defiles many. We hear about thousands of people who are killed in tribal and ethnic wars as a result of bitterness that took root years ago. We see churches divided and destroyed because of unresolved conflict between people who are brothers and sisters in Christ.

GROUP DISCUSSION. How would you describe a bitter person?

PERSONAL REFLECTION. How have you been affected by a root of bitterness in yourself or in another person?

No place in Scripture is there a clearer picture of a bitter spirit and its fruit of destruction than in the story of Herodias and John the Baptist. *Read Mark 6:14-29.*

1. We read about the miraculous things that Jesus and his disciples were doing in verses 12 and 13. What do you learn about Herod by his reactions to these miracles?

_____

2. What do you learn about John the Baptist?

_____

3. When have you had misperceptions about God or people because of guilt, anger or other emotions?

_____

4. Contrast Herod's reaction to John the Baptist with that of Herodias.

5. How do people in our culture usually respond to men and women who are truthful, righteous and holy?

6. How do you respond to someone who confronts you with the truth about yourself?

7. Verse 19 states that Herodias nursed a grudge against John. What is involved in "nursing" a grudge?

8. What more do you learn about Herodias from the sentence, "Finally the opportune time came" (v.21)?

9. Examine the request of Herodias and her daughter and the action of Herod. How is this a demonstration of the evil in the human heart and the power of bitterness?

10. How were each of the following affected by Herodias's grudge: Herod, Herodias, Herodias's daughter, John, John's disciples and the world?

11. What are alternatives to nursing a grudge?

12. What are the steps that you need to take to deal with grudges and bitterness in you?

Pray about the grudges in your heart that need to be given to God and forgiven. Ask him to weed out bitterness that is trying to or has taken root in your heart.

Now or Later

The next time you read a newspaper or newsmagazine, look for examples where bitterness has caused destruction. Pray for the people, the country and the parts of the world where you see it.

4

A Sinful Woman

A Forgiven Heart

Luke 7:36-50

I experience a sense of hopelessness when I am intensely aware of my depravity. Even despair. Darkness threatens to overcome me. I also know what it is to be forgiven by God and others. To experience the freedom of being released from my sin. To feel the exhilaration that comes from being loved completely and accepted for who I am.

GROUP DISCUSSION. How does it feel when you approach someone you have offended to ask for forgiveness?

PERSONAL REFLECTION. What does it mean to you to be forgiven?

In stark contrast to Herodias, who chose to be locked into her bitterness and sin, is another sinful woman who seeks and receives Jesus' forgiveness. *Read Luke 7:36-50.*

1. Compare and contrast how Simon the Pharisee and this woman would have been regarded by others.

2. Put yourself in the sandals of this sinful woman. Would you have entered Simon's house uninvited? Explain.

3. How do you feel as you enter Simon's house?

4. Describe the actions of the woman toward Jesus.

_____

5. Contrast Simon's attitude toward the woman (v.39) with Jesus' attitude toward her (vv.48-50).

_____

6 do you think Jesus receives you when you come to him in repentance?

_____

7What is the point of the story Jesus tells Simon in verses 41-43?

_____

8 Contrast the way Simon acted toward Jesus with the way the woman acted toward him (vv.44-47).

_____

9 How did these actions demonstrate the point of Jesus' story?

_____

10 How are you like Simon in your response to Jesus?

_____

How are you like the woman?

_____

11. How can you become more like the sinful woman in your love for Jesus?

_____

Ask God to give you a humble and repentant heart. Ask him to increase your awareness of how much he has forgiven you.

Now or Later

Review this passage again. List the external behaviors and internal responses of Simon the Pharisee. Next, make a column of Jesus' response to each response and behavior listed. Now make similar columns of the behaviors and responses of the woman and of Jesus' responses. What do you learn about Jesus from these observations? How do you respond to him?

5

The Canaanite Woman

Persevering in Prayer

Matthew 15:21-28

Sometimes when I pray I feel like the heavens are open and I can soar directly into God's presence. I know that he is there, eagerly waiting to respond to my words. At other times it feels like every approach to God goes no further than the ceiling and comes back down on my heavy soul. At these times persevering in prayer is hard work.

GROUP DISCUSSION. When have you felt discouraged because you thought God was ignoring your prayers?

PERSONAL REFLECTION. When have you seen God answer your request after long, difficult, persevering prayer?

In this passage we will look at the faith of the Canaanite woman, who persisted in prayer. *Read Matthew 15:21-28.*

1. How did those in this story respond to the Canaanite woman?

_____

2. How would you have felt if you had been treated this way?

_____

3. Why did the woman address Jesus as "Lord, Son of David" (v.22)?

_____

4. At this time there was tension between Jews and Gentiles, and women were not allowed to approach men. How would this dialogue be affected by each of these facts?

5. In what ways is the content of her prayer an excellent model of how we should approach Jesus (vv.22, 25, 27)?

6. What was Jesus' first reaction to her prayerful cry (v.23)?

7. How do you feel when someone responds to you in dead silence?

8. Describe the increasingly severe obstacles the woman faces as she continues to ask Jesus for help (vv.24-27).

_____

9. How did she respond to each?

_____

10. What does her reply in verse 27 suggest that she recognized?

_____

11. Jesus was pleased with her faith, and her request was granted. Describe what your prayer life is like when facing difficult, even seemingly hopeless situations.

_____

12. How would you like to grow in your prayer life?

Ask God to allow you to persevere in prayer as you see him more clearly and your confidence in him grows.

Now or Later

Look closely at the way that the Canaanite woman approached Jesus. How do you usually approach him? How does the way you approach him compare and contrast to her? What changes would you like to make in your approach to Jesus? in how you persevere in prayer?

6

Mary and Martha

Facing Death & Grief

John 11:1-44

The Sunday school lesson was about Jesus raising Lazarus from the dead. Jill was abrupt, typically honest and refreshing. "It isn't fair," she said. "When my friend dies, I have to deal with it. When Jesus' friend dies, he just raises him from the dead!" Though Jill's feelings were legitimate, there is much more to John 11. Jesus is not just avoiding the sting of death by raising his friend Lazarus from the dead.

GROUP DISCUSSION. How do you express personal grief?

PERSONAL REFLECTION. Consider your most painful loss. Journal about your feelings, how you expressed these feelings, how you felt about God and your relationship with him, and what was most helpful to you during that time.

In this passage we will see how Jesus related to Mary and Martha in their grief, experienced their sorrow as well as his own, comforted them and demonstrated his power over death, to the glory of God. *Read John 11:1-16.*

1. Describe Jesus' relationship with Mary, Martha and Lazarus.

2. If you were there as a disciple, how would his response to the news that Lazarus was sick (vv.4-6) be confusing to you in light of his close relationship with the family?

3. What are Jesus' primary objectives in this episode of Lazarus's sickness (vv.4, 14)?

4. To what degree is God's glory and believing him central in your life?

5.   How can you help others believe God and see some of his glory?

_____

6.   *Read John 11:17-44.* Compare and contrast the ways that Martha and Mary each responded to Jesus and he to them.

7.   What hope did Jesus offer to Martha (vv.21-27)?

_____

8.   How did Jesus comfort Mary (vv.32-37)?

_____

9.   How does each sister communicate that she believes Jesus?

_____

10.   In what ways have you received comfort and hope from Jesus?

_____

11.   Jesus wanted people to believe and wanted God to be glorified. What do you think it was like for them to see Lazarus come out of the grave?

12.   Because of the love between Jesus and Mary and Martha, they came to him honestly in their grief, and he ministered to them. Do you trust Jesus enough to be open and honest with him about your pain? Explain.

13.   Whenever we are vulnerable and open with people about our losses, there is potential for them to hurt us. Do you trust Jesus or others enough to share your grief and pain with them? Explain.

Talk to Jesus about your love relationship with him, and ask him to cause it to grow and deepen. Talk to him about pain that you are experiencing. Allow him to be your comfort and hope.

Now or Later

Write a letter to Jesus. Talk to him about what hurts you. Express your pain to him as specifically as possible. What losses have you experienced in your past or present? How would you like for him to walk through your pain with you? Tell him about when you have known his presence deeply. Thank him that he cares about what you are experiencing and for

being present in your grief. Praise him for his
hope and comfort.

7

Sapphira

Dishonest to God

Acts 4:32—5:11

I love the cartoon that shows a picture of an answering machine. When the phone rings, the recorded message says: "I am listening to your voice. If, when I hear you, I want to talk to you, I will pick up the telephone. Otherwise, leave a message." The caption under the cartoon says, "Finally, an honest answering machine."

Sometimes we find ourselves in Christian communities where dishonesty prevails. Rather than "speaking the truth in love" we talk about others behind their backs and, worse yet, sometimes in the form of prayer requests. Or we live double lives with an outward appearance of Christian behavior that barely disguises our fractured relationships, sexual sin and brokenness.

It is sad when it is only on rare occasions that we find ourselves saying, "Finally, an honest Christian."

GROUP DISCUSSION. How would you describe the level of honesty in churches, fellowships and Christian organizations you know?

PERSONAL REFLECTION. When you hear the words "being honest with God" what do you think about?

In this study we will consider how seriously God takes our being honest with him. *Read Acts 4:32-37.*

_____

1. What was the evidence that "all the believers were one in heart and mind"?

_____

2. What would it be like to be part of such a Christian community?

_____

3. *Read Acts 5:1-11.* All is not perfect, however, in the early church. How do the actions of Ananias and Sapphira (5:1-2) contrast with the actions of Barnabas (4:36-37)?

4.   Pretend that you are a news reporter and are watching the action between Peter and Ananias and Sapphira. How would you report it?

5.   What is the sin that Peter confronted (5:1-4)?

6.   In what ways are you tempted to lie to the Holy Spirit, other believers or yourself?

7.   Today the teaching that wives should submit to their husbands is sometimes distorted

to suggest that husbands are responsible for all the actions of their wives. How does Peter demonstrate that Sapphira is responsible to God for her own behavior (5:7-9)?

_____

8. How was the church affected by these startling deaths (5:11)?

_____

9. How does this story illustrate the high value that God places on truth?

_____

10. How does the practice of dishonesty in our Christian communities result in spiritual and emotional death?

11.   Up to this point in the book of Acts, Luke talks about attacks on the church from the outside. In this incident, however, the church comes under fire from within. How does this reveal the craftiness of Satan?

_____

12.   How do you see Satan attacking the Christian community from within today?

Pray for your own church and the church worldwide. Ask God to protect it from within and without—to give it great unity.

Now or Later

In a concordance look for passages of Scripture on honesty, truth and dishonesty. Read each of them and jot down the main truth or truths. As you go back over them, think about ways that you can become a more honest person.

8

Lydia

*A Businesswoman
Turns to Christ*

Acts 16:6-15

Sometimes we know that we have followed God's prompting. I have a vivid memory of such an occasion. The event was InterVarsity's Urbana Mission Conference. The place, a dormitory room. The person, a student who was in my small group Bible study.

I was walking down the hall when I sensed the prompting of the Holy Spirit to stop by Susan's room. As I walked in to say hello, she looked up from the booklet she was reading and said, "Will you help me to become a Christian?"

GROUP DISCUSSION. When is it easy for you to obey God? When is it difficult?

PERSONAL REFLECTION. Think about a time or situation in which you were particularly sensitive to the leading of the Holy Spirit. What was that like?

My journey to Susan's room was quite different from Paul's journey to meet Lydia, but the power of seeing the Lord open a heart to the message of the gospel is the same. *Read Acts 16:6-15.*

1. How is Paul directed to where he should go (vv.6-10)?

2. What principles of guidance do you see here?

3. When have you experienced God's leading in this way?

4. Paul and his companions arrived in Philippi on the Sabbath. They were looking for a place of prayer but, instead, found a gathering of women. What does their response tell us about their view of women?

_____

5. What do you discover about evangelism from verse 14?

6. How can the fact that it is the Lord who opens hearts to his message be a source of encouragement to you?

_____

7. What is the significance of the fact that a woman is the first convert in Europe?

8. Lydia was a leader in business, in the community and in her household. What contributions would she make to the church?

_____

9. Hospitality is one of the contributions Lydia made. It is directly spoken of in this passage (v.15). What difference would her hospitality make to Paul, Silas, Luke and the church?

10. How could the story of Lydia's conversion, leadership and contributions to the first church in Europe encourage women today who desire to be used by God in the church?

Pray that God will make us more faithful in hearing him, obeying him and reaching out to others with the good news of the gospel. Ask him to help us use our unique gifts for the furtherance of his kingdom.

Now or Later

For the next two weeks spend fifteen minutes each day in silence before the Lord. Ask him to give you ears to hear his voice and to know his mind for you. Ask him to make you constantly aware of his direction in your life.

9

Euodia and Syntyche

Women in Conflict

Philippians 3:20—4:9; 2:1-8

I trusted Betty. We had shared a lot of life: dormitory days in nursing school, difficult instructors, the death of Betty's grandfather, Betty's becoming a Christian, fun times and exciting Bible studies. She was one of the first people I had ever been vulnerable with.

We made plans to go back to college together to finish work on our degrees. Then suddenly Betty changed her mind. It was more convenient for her to stay where she was. I was hurt deeply. I felt unimportant to her, betrayed. The hurt then turned to anger and the unresolved anger to bitterness.

Because we were leaders in our fellowship group, many others felt the effects of our broken relationship. What had once been a bright testimony of sisters walking together in unity now became a slam to the gospel.

Through this experience, I learned very important lessons about relationships, resolving conflict and forgiveness.

GROUP DISCUSSION. How have you seen public conflict between leaders affect a church?

PERSONAL REFLECTION. How have you been affected by conflict in your life?

In this study we will see how seriously Paul viewed the leadership of two women and the conflict between them. *Read Philippians 3:20—4:3.*

1.   How does Paul feel about this church (4:1)?

2.   Paul instructs the Philippians to stand firm. What is the basis of this instruction (3:20-21)?

3.   How do you feel when you see conflict between your Christian brothers and sisters?

4. How seriously does Paul take the conflict between Euodia and Syntyche? Explain

5. What does Paul's deep concern say about the importance of Euodia and Syntyche, their influence in the church and their value to Paul?

6. Paul begged that the women would "agree with each other in the Lord." Earlier in this book Paul gave instructions about agreeing. *Read Philippians 2:1-8.* According to 2:1-2, why is it important for the Philippian Christians to be like-minded?

7. What can they do to be like-minded (2:3-5)?

_____

8. What does it mean to "do nothing out of selfish ambition" and to "in humility consider others better than yourself"?

_____

9. How was Jesus the perfect model of this in his life and in his death (2:6-8)?

_____

10. In what ways do you struggle with taking on Jesus' attitude?

11. How do you see yourself growing more like Jesus?

_____

12. *Read Philippians 4:4-9.* How would following each of these instructions contribute to unity among believers?

_____

13. What specific steps do you want to take in order to live out being a person of Christlike unity?

Ask God to make your heart tender toward those who are in conflict and cause you to grieve over disunity in the church. Ask him to make you sensitive to any wrong attitudes that you may have that lead to conflict with others. Ask him to give you a heart of repentance.

Now or Later

Carefully go back over Philippians 3:20—4:9; 2:1-8. Summarize the basis for standing firm in the Lord according to 3:20-21. Then list the practical instructions given in chapter 4. Next to each instruction write down how you need to integrate that directive into your life. Finally, write out a description of Jesus from Philippians 2:6-8. Describe how you want your attitude to become more like his.

10

Priscilla

A Partner in Leadership

Acts 18:1-4, 18-28

One of the greatest joys of my marriage is the partnership that Andy and I share. This is lived out in all sorts of ways. For instance, he enjoys the kitchen more than I do and adds creativity to our cooking. We raise kids together. I am responsible for taking care of the car. I pay the bills. He balances the checkbook. We also share leadership in ministry.

GROUP DISCUSSION. Describe a time when you have enjoyed sharing leadership in ministry with someone.

PERSONAL REFLECTION. What are your thoughts about couples sharing leadership in the church?

In this study we will observe a couple who led together in the church. *Read Acts 18:1-4.*

1. Describe the circumstances of the beginning of Paul's relationship with Aquila and Priscilla.

_____

2. If you were Paul, how do you think you would be affected by this kind of relationship?

_____

3. *Read Acts 18:18-28.* What advantages were there for Paul in having Aquila and Priscilla with him on this trip to Ephesus?

_____

4. If you were writing a recommendation for Apollos, how would you describe him (vv.24-25)?

5.   What did Aquila and Priscilla contribute to Apollos's spiritual journey?

6.   How have people encouraged your spiritual growth?

7.   What aspects of modern culture make it difficult to help someone in their spiritual growth?

8.   To whom might God be calling you to "explain the way of God more adequately"?

How do you feel about this responsibility?

_____

9. Look closely at the description of Apollos in verses 27-28. How do his qualities, experience and heritage prepare him for the ministry God had for him in Achaia?

10. What do you think are the advantages of a married couple or close friends sharing leadership in ministry today?

_____

11. *Read Romans 16:3-5 and 1 Corinthians 16:19.* What did Priscilla and Aquila contribute to Paul's life and the life of the church?

12.   How can you encourage leaders in their
        ministry?

       *Pray for the zeal and desire to obey God
that you see in Aquila and Priscilla. Ask God
to lead you to a person you can build into
spiritually and to make you faithful to that
person. Thank God for his faithfulness to you.*

Now or Later

Write a letter of appreciation and
encouragement to one or two Christian leaders
who have affected or are affecting your life.

Leader's Notes

MY GRACE IS SUFFICIENT FOR YOU. (2 COR 12:9)

Leading a Bible discussion can be an enjoyable and rewarding experience. But it can also be *scary*—especially if you've never done it before. If this is your feeling, you're in good company. When God asked Moses to lead the Israelites out of Egypt, he replied, "O Lord, please send someone else to do it!" (Ex 4:13). It was the same with Solomon, Jeremiah and Timothy, but God helped these people in spite of their weaknesses, and he will help you as well.

You don't need to be an expert on the Bible or a trained teacher to lead a Bible discussion. The idea behind these inductive studies is that the leader guides group members to discover for themselves what the Bible has to say. This method of learning will allow group members to remember much more of what is said than a lecture would.

These studies are designed to be led easily. As a matter of fact, the flow of questions through the passage from observation to interpretation to application is so natural that you may feel that the studies lead themselves. This study guide is also flexible. You can use it with a variety of groups—student, professional, neighborhood or church groups. Each study takes forty-five to sixty minutes in a group setting.

There are some important facts to know about group dynamics and encouraging discussion. The suggestions listed below should enable you to effectively and enjoyably fulfill your role as leader.

Preparing for the Study

1. Ask God to help you understand and apply the passage in your own life. Unless this happens, you will not be prepared to lead others. Pray too for the various members of the group. Ask God to open your hearts to the message of his Word and motivate you to action.

2. Read the introduction to the entire guide to get an overview of the entire book and the issues which will be explored.

3. As you begin each study, read and reread the assigned Bible passage to familiarize yourself with it.

4. This study guide is based on the New International Version of the Bible. It will help you and the group if you use this translation as the basis for your study and discussion.

5. Carefully work through each question in the study. Spend time in meditation and reflection as you consider how to respond.

6. Write your thoughts and responses in the space provided in the study guide. This will help you to express your understanding of the passage clearly.

7. It might help to have a Bible dictionary handy. Use it to look up any unfamiliar words, names or places. (For additional help on how to study a passage, see chapter five of *How to Lead a LifeGuide Bible Study*, InterVarsity Press.)

8. Consider how you can apply the Scripture to your life. Remember that the group will follow your lead in responding to the studies. They will not go any deeper than you do.

9. Once you have finished your own study of the passage, familiarize yourself with the leader's notes for the study you are leading. These are designed to help you in several ways. First, they tell you the purpose the study guide author had in mind when writing the study. Take time to think through how the study questions work together to accomplish that purpose. Second, the notes provide you with additional background information or suggestions on group dynamics for various questions. This information can be useful when people have difficulty understanding or answering a question. Third, the leader's notes can alert you to potential problems you may encounter during the study.

10. If you wish to remind yourself of anything mentioned in the leader's notes, make a note to yourself below that question in the study.

Leading the Study

1. Begin the study on time. Open with prayer, asking God to help the group to understand and apply the passage.

2. Be sure that everyone in your group has a study guide. Encourage the group to prepare beforehand for each discussion by reading the introduction to the guide and by working through the questions in the study.

3. At the beginning of your first time together, explain that these studies are meant to be discussions, not lectures. Encourage the members of the group to participate. However, do not put pressure on those who may be hesitant to speak during the first few sessions. You may want to suggest the following guidelines to your group.

☐ Stick to the topic being discussed.

☐ Your responses should be based on the verses which are the focus of the discussion and not on outside authorities such as commentaries or speakers.

☐ These studies focus on a particular passage of Scripture. Only rarely should you refer to other portions of the Bible. This allows for everyone to participate in in-depth study on equal ground.

☐ Anything said in the group is considered confidential and will not be discussed outside the group unless specific permission is given to do so.

☐ We will listen attentively to each other and provide time for each person present to talk.

☐ We will pray for each other.

4. Have a group member read the introduction at the beginning of the discussion.

5. Every session begins with a group discussion question. The question or activity is meant to be used before the passage is read. The question introduces the theme of the study and encourages group members to begin to open up. Encourage as many members as possible to participate, and be ready to get the discussion going with your own response.

This section is designed to reveal where our thoughts or feelings need to be transformed by Scripture. That is why it is especially important not to read the passage before the discussion question is asked. The passage will tend to color the honest reactions people would otherwise give because they are, of course, supposed to think the way the Bible does.

You may want to supplement the group discussion question with an icebreaker to help people to get comfortable. See the community section of *Small Group Idea Book* for more ideas.

You also might want to use the personal reflection question with your group. Either allow a time of silence for people to respond individually or discuss it together.

6. Have a group member (or members if the passage is long) read aloud the passage to be studied. Then give people several minutes to read the passage again silently so that they can take it all in.

7. Question I will generally be an overview question designed to briefly survey the passage. Encourage the group to look at the whole passage, but try to avoid getting sidetracked by questions or issues that will be addressed later in the study.

8. As you ask the questions, keep in mind that they are designed to be used just as they are written. You may simply read them aloud. Or you may prefer to express them in your own words.

There may be times when it is appropriate to deviate from the study guide. For example, a question may have already been answered. If so, move on to the next question. Or someone may raise an important question not covered in the guide. Take time to discuss it, but try to keep the group from going off on tangents.

9. Avoid answering your own questions. If necessary, repeat or rephrase them until they are clearly understood. Or point out something you read in the leader's notes to clarify the context or meaning. An eager group quickly becomes passive and silent if they think the leader will do most of the talking.

10. Don't be afraid of silence. People may need time to think about the question before formulating their answers.

11. Don't be content with just one answer. Ask, "What do the rest of you think?" or "Anything else?" until several people have given answers to the question.

12. Acknowledge all contributions. Try to be affirming whenever possible. Never reject an answer. If it is clearly off-base, ask, "Which verse led you to that conclusion?" or again, "What do the rest of you think?"

13. Don't expect every answer to be addressed to you, even though this will probably happen at first. As group members become more at ease, they will begin to truly interact with each other. This is one sign of healthy discussion.

14. Don't be afraid of controversy. It can be very stimulating. If you don't resolve an issue completely, don't be frustrated. Move on and keep it in mind for later. A subsequent study may solve the problem.

15. Periodically summarize what the group has said about the passage. This helps to draw together the various ideas mentioned and gives continuity to the study. But don't preach.

16. At the end of the Bible discussion you may want to allow group members a time of quiet to work on an idea under "Now or Later." Then discuss what you experienced. Or you may want to encourage group members to work on these ideas between meetings. Give an opportunity during the session for people to talk about what they are learning.

17. Conclude your time together with conversational prayer, adapting the prayer suggestion at the end of the study to your group. Ask for God's help in following through on the commitments you've made.

18. End on time.

Many more suggestions and helps are found in *How to Lead a LifeGuide Bible Study,* which is part of the LifeGuide Bible Study series.

Components of Small Groups

A healthy small group should do more than study the Bible. There are four components to consider as you structure your time together.

Nurture. Small groups help us to grow in our knowledge and love of God. Bible study is the key to making this happen and is the foundation of your small group.

Community. Small groups are a great place to develop deep friendships with other Christians. Allow time for informal interaction before and after each study. Plan activities and games that will help you get to know each other. Spend time having fun together—going on a picnic or cooking dinner together.

Worship and prayer. Your study will be enhanced by spending time praising God together in prayer or song. Pray for each other's needs—and keep track of how God is answering prayer in your group. Ask God to help you to apply what you are learning in your study.

Outreach. Reaching out to others can be a practical way of applying what you are learning, and it will keep your group from becoming self-focused. Host a series of evangelistic discussions for your friends or neighbors. Clean up the yard of an elderly friend. Serve at a soup kitchen together, or spend a day working on a Habitat house.

Many more suggestions and helps in each of these areas are found in *Small Group Idea Book.* Information on building a small group can be found in *Small Group Leaders' Handbook* and *The Big Book on Small Groups* (both from Inter-Varsity Press). Reading through one of these books would be worth your time.

Study 1. Elizabeth: Receiving God's Goodness. Luke 1:5-25, 39-45, 57-66.

Purpose: To see how Elizabeth's ability to receive God's goodness affected not only her relationship with God but that with her husband, neighbors and relatives.

General note. Every study begins with an "approach" question, which is meant to be asked before the passage is read. These questions are important for several reasons.

First, they help the group to warm up to each other. No matter how well a group may know each other, there is always a stiffness that needs to be overcome before people will begin to talk openly. A good question will break the ice.

Second, approach questions get people thinking along the lines of the topic of the study. Most people will have lots of different things going on in their minds (dinner, an important meeting coming up, how to get the car fixed) that will have nothing to do with the study. A creative question will get their attention and draw them into the discussion.

Third, approach questions can reveal where our thoughts or feelings need to be transformed by Scripture.

Question 1. This question is meant to help the group get to know Elizabeth. Feel free to add a couple of questions to lead them in discovering who she is. For example, "What do you think it means to be 'upright in the sight of God' (v.6)?" Or "How do you think Elizabeth felt about being childless?"

Question 2. Consider how unique John was. You might ask the group: What would be accomplished through him? How would people's lives be affected because of him? Elizabeth was receiving the goodness of God through John.

Questions 3-4. Keep in mind that we see Zechariah's reaction when he has just received the word from Gabriel out of the blue. Elizabeth is already pregnant in verse 25 where her response is described. However, we are all likely to be at different points when reminded of God's promises and goodness. These questions are meant to prepare the way for considering how others see God in our lives by the way we respond to his goodness.

Question 5. There are many reasons for not accepting good gifts from God. Disbelief and lack of trust are probably the greatest causes. These seem to be Zechariah's problems.

Question 6. What happens between Mary and Elizabeth is significant. Our Christian brothers and sisters are very important to what God is doing in our lives. It should be second nature to share our joys and sorrows with each other. In a world where doubts and questions and criticisms could be thrown at these women, they find community in each other. In the next study we'll look more at Mary's story in verses 26-38 and 46-56.

Question 7. Look closely at both this question and the passage. This question is not meant to just feed back the facts of what transpired between Elizabeth and Mary. It is meant to help the group look more deeply at sharing the thrill of God's work in their lives, confirming what God is doing and therefore building up one another's faith, testifying to the work of the Holy Spirit in each other, and encouraging and commending each other's faith and obedience.

Question 10. The neighbors, relatives and Elizabeth's husband all learned about God's great mercy through John's birth. They were able to see this and experience it because Elizabeth so freely received from God and mirrored his grace in her life.

Zechariah learned obedience and grew in faith. Saying "His name is John" was a direct act of obedience and humility. He experienced and knew God in a new way and learned more about praise.

The word about God spread. Everyone was talking about the events and seeing God working dramatically. They all learned to expect more from God based on what they had seen of him. They asked, "What then is this child going to be?" because they saw the Lord's hand with him and expected God to continue to work in and through him. Their faith was growing.

Question 11. Sometimes it is difficult for people to talk about the positive work that God is doing in them for fear of sounding proud or boastful. Encourage open conversation, giving God all the glory and praise. This discussion should be motivated by the responses to question 10. Hopefully your group will become excited by the possibilities of God's grace and mercy being seen in our lives, as it was in Elizabeth's.

Study 2. Mary: Believing the Impossible. Luke 1:26-38, 46-56.

Purpose: To observe Mary's faith. She not only believed that she, a virgin, would become pregnant by the Holy Spirit, but that her son's kingdom would last forever.

Question 1. You might want to set up a role play in which one person is Mary and another is her best friend. Encourage expression of excitement, fear and other feelings that Mary might have experienced. Be careful not to put anyone on the spot. Ask for volunteers.

Question 2. Help the group to think through all of the truth that Gabriel just told Mary: she has special favor with God; she is a virgin who will be with child conceived by the Holy Spirit, whose name has already been chosen; the child is the Son of God who will be given the throne of David and a kingdom that will never end.

Question 4. Although we did not concentrate on Zechariah in the last study, there is a contrast in his and Mary's response to Gabriel's messages. Help the group to discuss the perceived attitudes, content of the questions and general response to Gabriel. Discuss the difference in the response of Gabriel to each of them and what he perceived based on his response.

Question 9. This question is meant as an overview. Do not get hung up on too many details, and be aware of the time. It is a marvelous prayer. There are questions to follow that will get more into some of the details. Some of these questions may come up during this overview. No problem. Just skip the questions later in the study. The more the discussion flows from the group the better, as long as there is focus.

Question 10. Often we are caught up in our own little worlds and forget that our God is the God of history as well as the present. He has faithfully demonstrated his power and glory throughout history—and is the same God today. God is at work in the present, shaping our future.

Study 3. Herodias: The Fruit of Bitterness. Mark 6:14-29.

Purpose: To understand that the fruit of bitterness is destructive; being hardened to our sin can lead to greater sin.

Group Discussion. According to Scripture, bitterness seems to be the result of failing to depend on and respond to the grace of God. Though this is true and it begins in our relationship with God, bitterness then spreads throughout the community. Moses speaks of this in Deuteronomy 29:18 where he warns about one who turns his heart away from God to worship other gods and produces poison that affects the whole congregation.

When we turn our hearts away from the grace of God, we turn away from our brothers and sisters; bitterness can set in. As long as we have unresolved anger toward God or others, bitterness will continue. When Herodias was exposed to the grace of God through the life and ministry of John the Baptist, she became resentful and bitter toward John.

Question 4. This question will move your group through the whole passage. Though you are comparing two godless people, their responses to John are distinct. The outcome would have been totally different if Herod had really been in charge and gone with his inclinations. You could even wonder what would have happened to Herod spiritually if John had been allowed to stick around. Herod listened to him though he found him puzzling.

There are a lot of issues that come up by contrasting these two individuals: response to truth, manipulation, being controlled by fleshly pleasures, peer pressure and the effect of sin on innocent people. Help the group to discover these.

Questions 6. The depth of discussion will depend on the comfort of the group members with each other and the degree to which they choose to be vulnerable. Lead sensitively and carefully. If needed to prompt discussion, allow or encourage people to speak in the third person.

Question 8. Verse 19 says that she wanted to kill him. This phrase demonstrates her waiting to seize the opportunity to do so. She was obsessed with evil. Murder of a just man was her revenge. She did not hesitate to take the opportunity.

Question 10. This question is meant to demonstrate the wide effects of bitterness. If the group has trouble noting how the world was affected, you could rephrase the question: How do you think the death of John affected the world around him?

Question 11. Do not let the group pass over this lightly. Work hard at thinking through alternatives to nursing a grudge.

Question 12. Remind the group that dealing with not forgiving others, carrying grudges and nursing those grudges is common to all of us, and so practical steps are helpful in finding our way through.

Study 4. A Sinful Woman: A Forgiven Heart. Luke 7:36-50.

Purpose: To observe what it means to receive Jesus' forgiveness and to love much as a result of being forgiven much.

Question 1. The whole town knew that the woman had lived a sinful life. In the eyes of society, Simon was the religious leader and would appear to be spiritually superior to this woman.

Questions 2-3. Consider the strikes she had against her (socially, culturally, psychologically, spiritually). She was in a culture which did not respect or value women. She had a bad reputation in the community. She was not considered religious. All of this could have caused her to feel very self-conscious and insecure. On the other hand, though her actions would be considered inappropriate by most, she might not have cared about what people thought because she was under so much emotional stress.

There is certainly no right or wrong answer to these questions, but hopefully the group will enter into the situation more by thinking about this woman's feelings.

Question 6. This question about how we "think" Jesus receives us is significant because many are either afraid to approach Jesus for forgiveness or do not feel forgiven by him after they do. Talking about how we approach Jesus, what we receive from him, how we feel about what we receive and our doubts about being forgiven can help. There are possibly some in the group who do not feel they need Jesus' forgiveness. If this is true it can lead to another whole kind of discussion.

Question 7. The basic point of this parable is that the more a person is forgiven, the more they love. However, we need to acknowledge that sin is sin. The more we are aware of the depravity in us, the more we love.

Question 10. The response to this question can be twofold. The group can talk about where they are in general or where they are today in their sense of sinfulness and love or lack thereof for Jesus.

Study 5. The Canaanite Woman: Persevering in Prayer. Matthew 15:21-28.

Purpose: To learn that we should continue to confidently make our requests known to God because he responds to perseverance in prayer.

Question 1. Make sure the group knows that the fact that the woman is a Canaanite is significant because (1) she is Gentile and (2) the Canaanites were the traditional enemies of Israel in the Old Testament.

Question 3. Addressing Jesus as the Son of David, the Canaanite woman acknowledged that Jesus was the Jewish Messiah.

Question 4. Look at this question from both Jesus' and the woman's perspective. The issue of defilement now recurs in a more practical form. Jesus, the Jewish teacher, had moved into Gentile territory and was confronted by a Gentile woman with a demon-possessed daughter. The dialogue which resulted focused on the question of how far a Gentile might expect any benefit from the Jewish Messiah *(Son of David)* (D.A. Carson, R.T. France, J.A. Motyer and G.J. Wenham, eds., *New Bible Commentary, 21st Century Edition* [Downers Grove, Ill.: InterVarsity Press, 1994], p.924).

Question 5. She makes a clear statement of who Jesus is and of her confidence in him. She cries for mercy, which acknowledges her helplessness. And then she clearly states her need.

Question 8. Already (vv.22-23) she has faced two severe obstacles to her prayer being answered. She is met with silence from the one she addresses in her need. And then his disciples tell him to send her away. When Jesus does respond, it seems he eliminates any hope by saying clearly that he was sent *only* to the sheep of Israel. And finally he is even more wounding by comparing Gentiles with dogs—unclean animals.

The *New Bible Commentary* notes that Jesus' language may seem harsh. "Perhaps cold print conceals an element of irony, even playfulness, in Jesus' tone. At any rate, he was confronting her with the sort of language a Gentile could expect to hear from a Jew" (pp.924-25).

Question 10. "Her reply in verse 27 recognizes the priority of his mission to Israel but, nonetheless, claimed an extension of that mission to Gentiles. She had thus perceived the plan to which God had been working ever since the call of Abraham (Gen. 12:1-3), and which would in due time extend the church outside the bounds of Israel" (*New Bible Commentary*, p.925).

Study 6. Mary and Martha: Facing Death & Grief. John 11:1-44.

Purpose: To grow in love and trust of God as we see Jesus minister to people who are in grief and demonstrate God's glory and power over death.

General Note. As the leader, you need to be aware that there may be people in your group who are grieving. The source could be a death, the loss of a job, a broken friendship or a wayward child. There is potential for deep feelings to be expressed. Listen long and hard. Direct the group to Jesus in this passage. Do not give easy answers. Grief can take a long time—people will not just get over it. If you or your group members want to do more study in this area, consider studying *Receiving Comfort from God* by Dale and Juanita Ryan.

Question 3. Throughout this passage Jesus' main concerns are that his disciples learn to believe (vv.14, 26, 40, 42) and that God is glorified (vv.4, 40).

Questions 4-5. Help the group to grapple with Jesus' concerns that God would be glorified and that people would believe. Discuss the issue of the centrality of God's glory and believing

Jesus in our lives and in our thinking. How important is it to us to believe Jesus and to live out his glory? How important to us is the condition of others' belief and whether they recognize his glory?

Question 6. This is an overview question for all these verses. Questions 7, 8 and 9 help fill in the details. Don't repeat questions that were answered adequately in the overview.

Some important principles: Jesus met Mary and Martha where they were emotionally and according to their individual personalities. He knew them and responded to them sensitively. They responded differently and communicated their faith differently, and this was accepted by Jesus.

Question 8. It might be hard to see Jesus comforting Mary rather than just getting the sense of the depth of his grief. Note the ways he comforted her: (1) He did not try to defend himself or explain why he wasn't there. He listened and took her seriously. (2) He felt with her in silence. (3) He allowed himself to express his own emotions. (4) He did not get distracted by defending himself to the crowd. Some of them questioned his love for Lazarus. "Could not he who opened the eyes of the blind man have kept this man from dying?" (v.37). Jesus kept his attention on Mary.

Question 10. This is not a "should" question but one in which you want your group members to freely and honestly express where they are in trusting Jesus with their pain. Some in your group may not feel Jesus was there to comfort and give hope when they needed him. Provide an environment that is safe and encourage honesty. People cannot grow in their trust and love relationship with Jesus if they are not allowed to honestly look at where they are and where they want to go.

Questions 12-13. It would be good for you to be ready to share specifics in response to these two questions. Don't be afraid of silence. These are personal questions. The responses are not necessarily easy to identify or articulate. Time in silence to think is important.

Study 7. Sapphira: Dishonest to God. Acts 4:32—5:11.

Purpose: To look closely at what it means to be honest with God, others and ourselves, to see how seriously God takes dishonesty, and to see that God holds women responsible for their actions.

Question 2. This question is not meant to foster discouragement about the churches that the members attend. It is meant to establish what an effective church might look and feel like.

Question 4. Help the group get into the story by reporting it as if they were eyewitnesses to the event.

Question 5. It is very clear that Ananias and Sapphira had a choice about what to do with their possessions. *The IVP Women's Bible Commentary* notes, "Peter makes it clear that they had the right to sell or not to sell the property, just as they had the right to give or not to give the proceeds (Acts 5:3-4)" (ed. Catherine Clark Kroeger and Mary Evans [Downers Grove, Ill.: InterVarsity Press, 2002], p.611). They were not punished for keeping some of the money. They were punished for lying to the Holy Spirit.

Question 6. Sometimes we are dishonest when we don't even realize it. Careful scrutiny is vital in our walk with God. Consider all three parts of this question. It is fairly personal so allow people to answer with general statements.

Question 7. *The IVP Women's Bible Commentary* highlights the significance of the fact that Sapphira had to take responsibility for her dishonesty:

> In a day when almost any wife could excuse herself on the grounds that she had no freedom to do other than obey her husband, Peter insists that she may not hide behind her husband's leadership. When it comes to moral and spiritual issues a wife must put the Lord's requirements before her husband's. (p.612)

Study 8. Lydia: A Businesswoman Turns to Christ. Acts 16:6-15.

Purpose: To observe how gender barriers continue to be broken down and the important role women played in the early church.

Question 2. Help your group to think through what it means to be guided by God. It is important to be willing at any time to lay aside our own plans, as good and well intentioned as they may be, in response to the Spirit's prompting. Though Paul had a thoughtful plan of action and travel, he changed it without apparent question when told by the Spirit on two different occasions not to go preach somewhere. Thoughtful plans are good, and God leads us in those plans as we are open to him.

Other principles of guidance are: asking God to open and close doors of circumstances to lead you; praying continually about plans and direction, and asking God to keep you in tune with his plans and in earshot of his voice. Be ready for God to speak to you in whatever way he chooses. Trust him to lead you both in the direction that he wants you to take as well as away from the wrong situations. And finally, obey immediately. It is in obedience that his guidance is confirmed and further direction given.

Questions 5-6. The principle of evangelism is that it is God who gives the increase. It is God who opens and changes hearts. It is God who prepares hearts for the message of Christ. This principle should make us more dependent on God and more prayerful in regards to evangelism. It should help us to relax and trust him for the work he wants to do. It should motivate us to faithfulness in proclaiming truth. It relieves us from pressuring anyone to respond to the gospel. We simply need to invite them.

Question 7. This question is not meant to make a big issue of a woman being the first convert. In a culture in which women were not well regarded it is simply a radical contrast to what would have been expected. Just as God elevates the poor, children and other cultural minorities, in this passage we see that women are significant to God.

Question 9. Offering hospitality and partnership became a tradition in the church of Philippi (Phil 1:5; 4:10), perhaps as a result of Lydia's leadership.

Study 9. Euodia and Syntyche: Women in Conflict. Philippians 3:20—4:9; 2:1-8.

Purpose: To look at how seriously Paul viewed the leadership of Euodia and Syntyche and the conflict between them. To grow in resolving conflict by taking on the mind of Christ.

Question 1. Paul loved the church at Philippi! Instead of causing him problems or criticizing him, they were his joy and delight. Yet Paul was concerned about two women, women who had worked by his side for the cause of the gospel. They were having difficulty getting along. He begged them to work through this conflict because their leadership was important to him and to the church.

There is much emotion expressed in 4:1. Help the group to understand Paul's feelings for this church by looking at each phrase and what it expresses—"my brothers," "you whom I love and long for," "my joy," "my crown."

The *New Bible Commentary* says, "The words here show the depth of Paul's feeling as he wrote to his friends at Philippi. Twice in the verse he uses the word which literally means 'beloved.' He rejoices in them. He sees them like a crown on his head.... More than anything else, he encourages them to *stand firm in the Lord* ... like soldiers determined not to be made to retreat whatever the forces against them" (pp. 1257-58).

Question 2. Whenever you see a "therefore" in Scripture, it is important to look back for the "why for" (the explanation). Here are one scholar's thoughts on why these instructions were given.

The thought of those whose lives are dominated by the desire for *earthly things* leads the apostle to say that true Christians know that their life and *citizenship* is even now in heaven with Christ.... Philippians could be proud of their citizenship in a Roman colony (see the Introduction), just as we all have an earthly citizenship which has its privileges and its obligations. But they, and we, have to value above all the gift of a heavenly life and citizenship, and we live in hope of our future inheritance that we will receive in its fullness in the future. Thus *we eagerly await* the reappearing from heaven of our *Savior, the Lord Jesus Christ.*

Christ's coming will mean the transformation of our *lowly bodies* to be *like his glorious body* ... by the power of God to whose working there can ultimately be no limitation or hindrance. The body that we have is not despised, but it is a sign of our present *lowly* condition.... Now our bodies are subject to pain and suffering and weakness; then they will be raised to be immortal and imperishable. (*New Bible Commentary*, p.1257)

The instruction to stand firm is based on the hope that our citizenship is in heaven, that we are waiting for the return of a Savior who has the power to transform and bring everything under his control. So, though the battle may get rough here and we may be tempted to give up, we have every reason to stand firm.

Question 3. Consider the possibilities of feeling judgment, pride or hardness toward others. Talk about what our response should be—humility, grief, desire for resolution and so on.

Question 10. As in all application questions, especially those that might be difficult, it helps to provide an environment for openness by talking about your own struggles. There is great richness in considering and aiming toward making Christ's mind our own.

Question 12. Hopefully there will be good discussion following the overview of verses 4-9 regarding how each affects unity.

Study 10. Priscilla: A Partner in Leadership. Acts 18:1-4, 18-28.

Purpose: To observe a couple who are leaders in the church and serve equally in the ministry.

Question 2. We are looking at a very important time in Paul's life. When he met Aquila and Priscilla, he met lifelong friends. We do not know how long it was before Paul realized this, but I would suspect that he was very aware of the great gift that they were to him. Not only were Aquila and Priscilla a support to Paul in his spiritual ministry, but they offered him a home. They also had much in common. This included the occupation of tentmaking, the fact that they were Jews and Christians, and that they were not residents of Corinth.

You have probably heard the term *tentmaking* used in Christian circles in regards to missions or ministry. This is where that term originates—Paul supported himself financially as a tentmaker while he ministered at Corinth (v.3). His relationship with Aquila and Priscilla was a means for him to easily use this occupation as a source of income.

Question 3. Besides the obvious benefit of company and support on this trip, he was able to leave them at Ephesus to oversee the ministry there while he continued his journey to strengthen the disciples elsewhere.

Question 4. According to the *New Bible Commentary*, "Alexandria in Egypt was among the most important cities in the Roman Empire. The large Jewish population there had a reputation for scholarly pursuits, producing both the influential Greek translation of the OT called the Septuagint and the great philosopher Philo. Apollos, *a learned man with a thorough knowledge of the Scriptures,* may have seen himself in this tradition" (pp.1095-96).

Lead the group through the description of Apollos and create a list of his good qualities. You will be discussing that list more thoroughly in question 9.

Question 5. "That Priscilla and Aquila, on hearing Apollos, *explained to him the way of God more accurately* implies that though his teaching was accurate (25), it was based on incomplete knowledge" (*New Bible Commentary*, p.1096).

Question 7. In this day of "success based on numbers" the tremendous vision of "making disciples" by investing time and energy in individuals may be lost. Two mature Christians gave time and energy to one person who, in time, was effective in reaching many others with the message of Christ.

Phyllis J. Le Peau is an area director with InterVarsity Christian Fellowship in Chicago. Phyllis authored Woman of Rest *and the LifeGuide® Bible Studies* Acts *and* Love. *With her husband, Andy, she coauthored the LifeGuides* Ephesians *and* James. *Over 500,000 LifeGuides by Phyllis LePeau have been sold. She is also the author of three Fruit of the Spirit Guides (Zondervan). She is the mother of four adult children.*

What Should We Study Next?

A good place to continue your study of Scripture would be with a book study. Many groups begin with a Gospel such as *Mark* (20 studies by Jim Hoover) or *John* (26 studies by Douglas Connelly). These guides are divided into two parts so that if twenty or twenty-six weeks seems like too much to do at once, the group can feel free to do half and take a break with another topic. Later you might want to come back to it. You might prefer to try a shorter letter. *Philippians* (9 studies by Donald Baker), *Ephesians* (11 studies by Andrew T. and Phyllis J. Le Peau) and *1 & 2 Timothy and Titus* (11 studies by Pete Sommer) are good options. If you want to vary your reading with an Old Testament book, consider *Ecclesiastes* (12 studies by Bill and Teresa Syrios) for a challenging and exciting study.

There are a number of interesting topical LifeGuide studies as well. Here are some options for filling three or four quarters of a year:

Basic Discipleship

Christian Beliefs, 12 studies by Stephen D. Eyre
Christian Character, 12 studies by Andrea Sterk & Peter Scazzero
Christian Disciplines, 12 studies by Andrea Sterk & Peter Scazzero

Evangelism, 12 studies by Rebecca Pippert & Ruth Siemens

Building Community

Fruit of the Spirit, 9 studies by Hazel Offner
Spiritual Gifts, 12 studies by Charles & Anne Hummel
Christian Community, 10 studies by Rob Suggs

Character Studies

David, 12 studies by Jack Kuhatschek
New Testament Characters, 12 studies by Carolyn Nystrom
Old Testament Characters, 12 studies by Peter Scazzero
Women of the Old Testament, 12 studies by Gladys Hunt

The Trinity

Meeting God, 12 studies by J.I. Packer
Meeting Jesus, 13 studies by Leighton Ford
Meeting the Spirit, 10 studies by Douglas Connelly

www.ingramcontent.com/pod-product-compliance
Lightning Source LLC
Chambersburg PA
CBHW011156090426
42740CB00019B/3401